Viking Cookbook © 2019 Alessandra Luciano. All Rights Reserved.

ISBN-13: 978-1-948909-525

Thirty-Three & 1/3 Publishing

Printed in the USA

Disclaimer.

No part of this book shall be reproduced, stored in a retrieval system, or transmitted by any means without written permission from the author.

The author does not in any way provide a guarantee or a warranty, express or implied, towards the content of recipes in this book. It is the reader's responsibility to determine the value and quality of
any recipe or instructions provided for food preparation and to
determine the nutritional value for yourself, if any, and safety of the preparation instructions.

The recipes presented are intended for educational, informational and entertainment purposes and for use by persons having appropriate technical skill, at their own discretion and risk. Further, the author is not liable, not responsible and does not assume obligation for:

- Adverse reactions to food consumed such as food poisoning and any kind of food-borne disease
- Misinterpreted recipe
- Domestic accidents, including but not limited to fires in your
- kitchen or cuts for example.
- Any food related allergic reactions you could have when
- trying a new food.
- Any alcohol related accidents that could occur when
- consuming alcohol. Do not ever drink and drive anything.

The author does not make any warranties for the outcome of your food experiments. Before trying a new recipe, make sure you or your family member is not allergic to any of the ingredients. Use the right amounts and tools. What you decide to do with the recipes here is your responsibility.

for my brother Jimmy

Recipe Index

Soups & Slow Cooker — 11

13	Potato, Pea & Leek Soup
15	Crockpot Chili
17	Crockpot Beef Stew
19	Crockpot Chicken Tacos
21	Crockpot Sloppy Joes
21	Slow Cooker Beef Pot Roast

Make Ahead Meals — 25

27	Freezer Shrimp Stir Fry
29	Freezer Chicken & Rice

Meat — 31

33	Loco Moco Hamburger & Egg
35	Whole Roasted Chicken
37	Shepherd's Pie

39   Jambalaya

41   Meat Loaf

Fish   43

45   Salmon, Spinach & White Beans

47   Baked Fish

49   Tuna Noodle Casserole

Salad   51

53   Cucumber Salad

55   Caprese Salad

57   Three Bean Salad

Sides   59

61   Mashed Potatoes

63   Mac Salad

65   Rice

67   Zucchini, Tomatoes & Onions

69   Oven Roasted Squash

71   Baked Potatoes

73   Baked Sweet Potatoes

Sandwiches   75

77   Egg Salad Sandwiches

79   Hard Boiled Eggs

81   Tuna Salad

Pasta   83

85   Lasagna

87   Spaghetti

89   Penne with Zucchini

91   Pasta Primavera

Breakfast Anytime   93

95   Potatoes with Spinach and Eggs

Desserts   97

99   Baked Rice Pudding

101   Peanut Butter Cookies

Venison   103

105   Stove Top Venison Chili

107   Slow Cooker Venison Roast

109   Slow Cooker Venison BBQ Sandwiches

111   Venison Cheeseburger Soup

113   Venison Taco Pie

115   Venison Sliders

117   Venison Bolognese

119   Venison Stroganoff

Soups & Slow Cooker

Potato, Pea & Leek Soup

Ingredients

8 potatoes, peeled and cubed
1 small package frozen peas
4 cups chicken broth
1 pound bacon, cut into 1 inch pieces (optional)
3 leeks, sliced
1 cup heavy cream
1 Tablespoon of Dill (optional)

Instructions

In a large saucepan or stockpot, bring potatoes and chicken broth to a boil.

Cook until potatoes are tender.

Meanwhile, place bacon in a

large, deep skillet. Cook over

medium high heat until evenly

brown.

Drain, reserving 3 tablespoons of grease and set

aside.

Sautee the leeks in the frying pan with the reserved bacon grease 8 to 10 minutes.

When the potatoes are tender, stir in the fried leeks, peas, heavy cream, bacon (optional) and dill (optional).

Stir to blend and remove from heat. Serve hot.

Crockpot Chili

Ingredients

1 pound browned ground beef
2 cans dark kidney beans
1 can (14.5 ounce) tomato sauce
1 can (14.5 ounce) crushed or diced tomatoes
1 packet of chili seasoning
2 cups of water

Instructions

Brown the meat in the frying pan.

After beef is browned, and grease drained, place in crockpot.

Add in kidney beans, tomato sauce, tomatoes, chili seasoning and water.

Stir until well combined.

Cook on LOW for 6-7 hours or HIGH for 4 hours.

Crockpot Beef Stew

Ingredients

1 pounds of stew meat, cut into 1-inch pieces
1/4 cup all-purpose flour
1/2 teaspoon salt
1/2 teaspoon ground black pepper
1 clove garlic, minced
1 bay leaf
1 teaspoon paprika
1 teaspoon Worcestershire sauce
1 onion, chopped
1- 1/2 cups beef broth
3 potatoes, diced
4 carrots, sliced
1 stalk celery, chopped

Instructions

Place meat in slow cooker. In a small bowl mix together the flour, salt, and pepper; pour over meat, and stir to coat meat with flour mixture. Stir in the garlic, bay leaf, paprika, Worcestershire sauce, onion, beef broth, potatoes, carrots, and celery.

Cover, and cook on Low setting for 10 to 12 hours, or on High setting for 4 to 6 hours.

Crockpot Chicken Tacos

Ingredients

2 Chicken Breast
1 Taco mild seasoning mix
1 can mild Ro-Tel tomatoes
Taco Shells or Tortillas
Taco Cheese
Sour Cream
Diced Tomatoes

Instructions

Put the whole chicken breast into crock pot

Pour taco seasoning packet over chicken breast

Pour can of mild Ro-Tel tomatoes over chicken and seasoning

Cover and cook 4-6 hours on high or 6-8 on low

About an hour before it's finished cooking use a large spoon to shred the chicken in the crock pot.

Serve in hard or soft taco shells and top with your favorite taco toppings.

Crockpot Sloppy Joes

Ingredients

1 teaspoon vegetable oil
1 1/2 pounds lean ground beef
1/2 medium yellow onion, finely chopped
1 medium red bell pepper, cored, seeded, and diced
1 (15-ounce) can tomato sauce
1/2 cup ketchup
2 tablespoons packed brown sugar
1 teaspoon Worcestershire sauce
1 teaspoon dry ground mustard
1/2 teaspoon garlic powder or minced garlic
1/2 teaspoon salt
1/4 teaspoon black pepper
Hamburger buns

Instructions

Brown the meat on the stovetop. Heat the oil in a large frying pan over medium-high heat until shimmering. Add the ground beef and use a stiff spatula or wooden spoon to break the meat into small pieces. Cook, stirring occasionally, until browned and no longer pink, 8 to 10 minutes.

Add the ingredients to the slow cooker. Transfer the browned ground beef to a 4-quart or larger slow cooker. Add the onions, bell pepper, tomato sauce, ketchup, brown sugar, Worcestershire, mustard, garlic powder, salt, and pepper. Stir until well-combined, making sure to break up the beef.

Slow cook the Sloppy Joes. Cover and cook on the LOW setting low for 4 to 8 hours, or on HIGH setting for 2 to 3 hours.

Slow Cooker Beef Pot Roast

Ingredients

1 beef pot roast (can also use venison or pork)
salt and pepper to taste
1 tablespoon all-purpose flour, or as needed
2 tablespoons vegetable oil
8 ounces sliced mushrooms
1 medium onion, chopped
2 tablespoons minced garlic
1 tablespoon butter
1 1/2 tablespoons all-purpose flour
1 tablespoon tomato paste
2 1/2 cups chicken broth
3 medium carrots, cut into chunks
2 stalks celery, cut into chunks
1 teaspoon dried rosemary (optional)
1-1/2 teaspoon dried thyme (optional)

Instructions

Generously season both sides of roast with salt and pepper. Sprinkle flour over the top until well coated, and pat it into the meat. Shake off any excess.

Heat vegetable oil in a large skillet over medium-high heat until hot. Sear the roast on both sides for 5-6 minutes each, until well browned. Remove from the skillet and set aside.

Reduce the heat to medium and stir in mushrooms and butter; cook for 3-4 minutes.

Stir in onion; cook for 5 minutes, until onions are translucent and begin to brown. Add garlic, stir for about a minute.

Stir in 1 1/2 tablespoons flour; cook and stir for about 1 minute. Add tomato paste, and cook for another minute.

Slowly add chicken stock, stir to combine, and return to a simmer. Remove skillet from the heat.

Place carrots and celery in the slow cooker. Place roast over the vegetables and pour in any accumulated juices. Add rosemary and thyme.

Pour onion and mushroom mixture over the top of the roast. Cover slow cooker, turn to high and cook the roast for 5-6 hours, until the meat is fork tender.

Skim off any fat from the surface and remove the bones. Season with salt and pepper to taste.

Make Ahead Dump Meals

Shrimp Stir Fry Freezer Pack

Ingredients

1 ½ - 2 pounds medium shrimp, peeled and deveined
1 bell pepper, chopped
1 cup sugar snap peas
2 carrots, peeled and grated
16 ounces broccoli florets
1 tablespoon olive oil
1 teaspoon sesame seeds
1 green onion, thinly sliced

For the Sauce later

3 tablespoons reduced sodium soy sauce
2 tablespoons oyster sauce
1 tablespoon rice wine vinegar
1 tablespoon brown sugar, packed
1 tablespoon freshly grated ginger
3 cloves garlic, minced
1 teaspoon sesame oil
1 teaspoon cornstarch

Instructions

In a large bowl, whisk together soy sauce, oyster sauce, vinegar, sugar, ginger, garlic, sesame oil, cornstarch. Stir in shrimp and gently toss to combine. In a gallon size Ziploc bag or large bowl, combine shrimp mixture, bell pepper, snap peas, carrots and broccoli. Place in freezer for up to 1 month.

Cooking Later: Heat olive oil in a large skillet over medium high heat. Add shrimp mixture, and cook, stirring occasionally, until shrimp is cooked through and vegetables are tender, about 8-10 minutes.

Freezer to Slow Cooker Cilantro Lime Chicken with Rice

Ingredients

1 1/2 pounds boneless, skinless chicken breasts
1 (15-ounce) can black beans, drained and rinsed
1 (10-ounce can) Ro-Tel Tomatoes
1 cup corn kernels, frozen, canned or roasted
1/2 cup salsa
1/2 cup chopped cilantro leaves
1 red onion, diced
1 jalapeño, diced
2 teaspoons cumin
2 teaspoons chili powder
4 cloves garlic, minced
Salt and black pepper, to taste
Juice of 2 limes
2 Cups Cooked Rice

Instructions

In a gallon size Ziploc bag or large bowl, combine chicken, beans, tomatoes, corn, salsa, cilantro, onion, jalapeno, cumin, chili powder and garlic. Place in freezer for up to 1 month.

Place chicken mixture into a 6-qt slow cooker; season

with salt and pepper, to taste. Cover and cook on low heat for 7-8 hours or high heat for 3-4 hours. Stir in lime juice.

Cook Rice on stove or in Rice Cooker. Service over cooked rice.

NOTE: *Thaw chicken mixture the night before in the refrigerator prior to adding to the slow cooker.

Meat

Loco Moco Hamburger with Egg

Ingredients

Cooking spray
1 pound ground beef or ground Turkey, Venison or Chicken
1 cup sliced onion
1 small package mushrooms
1/2 cup water
1 (12 ounce) jar brown gravy
4 eggs
2 cups cooked rice

Instructions

Cook the rice in the rice cooker.

Divide ground chuck into 4 equal portions; form into patties.

Stir onion and water into the reserved drippings. Reduce heat to
low and cook until the onions are slightly softened, about 5 minutes.

Pour gravy over the onion and mushroom mixture; stir. Cook until the gravy is hot, about 5 minutes.

Add hamburger patties to the frying pan.

While the patties simmer in gravy, fry two - four eggs over easy.

Put rice in a bowl, put hamburger patty on top, put the gravy over that and then add the egg last on top.

Whole Roasted Chicken

Ingredients

1 whole chicken, giblets removed salt and black pepper to taste
1 tablespoon onion powder
1/2 cup butter, divided
2 stalks celery

Instructions

Preheat oven to 350 degrees F

Place chicken in a roasting pan, and season generously inside and out with salt and pepper. Sprinkle inside and out with onion powder. Place 3 tablespoons butter in the chicken cavity.

Arrange dollops of the remaining butter around the chicken's exterior. Cut the celery into 3 or 4 pieces, and place in the chicken cavity.

Bake uncovered 1 hour and 15 minutes in the preheated oven, to a minimum internal temperature of 180 degrees F. Remove from heat and basted with melted butter and drippings. Cover with aluminum foil, and allow the bird to rest for about 30 minutes before serving.

Shepherd's Pie

Ingredients

2 pounds potatoes (about 4 large potatoes), peeled and quartered
1 stick butter
1 medium onion, chopped
1 bag frozen mixed vegetables (carrots, corn, peas)
1 pound ground round beef
½ cup beef broth
1 teaspoon Worcestershire sauce
Salt and pepper

Instructions

Boil the potatoes. Place the peeled and quartered potatoes in medium sized pot. Cover with at least an inch of cold water. Add a teaspoon of salt. Bring to a boil, reduce to a simmer, and cook until tender (about 20 minutes).

Cook the vegetables: While the potatoes are cooking, melt half the butter in a large sauté pan on medium heat. Add the chopped onions and cook until tender, about 6 to 10 minutes.   If you are including vegetables, add them after onions are cooked.

Add the ground beef, then Worcestershire sauce and broth. Add ground beef to the pan with the onions and vegetables. Cook until no longer pink. Season with salt and pepper.

Add the Worcestershire sauce and beef broth. Bring the broth to a simmer and reduce heat to low. Cook uncovered for 10 minutes, adding more beef broth if necessary to keep the meat from drying out.

Mash the cooked potatoes. When the potatoes are done cooking (a fork can easily pierce), remove them from the pot and place them in a bowl with the remaining half of the butter. Mash with a fork or potato masher, and season with salt and pepper to taste.

Layer the meat mixture and mashed potatoes in a casserole dish: Preheat oven to 400°F.

Spread the beef, onions, and vegetables (if using) in an even layer in a large baking dish (8x13 casserole). Spread the mashed potatoes over the top of the ground beef. Rough up the surface of the mashed potatoes with a fork so there are peaks that will get well browned.

Bake in oven at 400°F oven, cook until browned and bubbling, about 30 minutes.

Jambalaya

Ingredients

½ pound Bacon, Diced
1 pound Kielbasa Polish Sausage
1 pound Shrimp, peeled and deveined
3 tablespoons oil
2-4 skinless chicken breast cut unto cubes
Salt and Pepper
1 large onion. Chopped
1 green bell pepper, diced
3 celery stalks, diced
2 cups cooked rice
3 tablespoons minced garlic
2 bay leaves
1-1/2 tablespoons Paprika
1 teaspoon ground red pepper
1 tablespoon celery salt
1 small can crushed tomatoes
1 carton chicken stock
1 bunch green onions, chopped

Instructions

Cook 2 cups of rice.

Cook bacon, sausage and oil in hot pot, stirring slowly

with a long wooden spoon, for 10 minutes. Season chicken with salt and pepper.

Add the chicken to the pot, cook about 5 minutes until brown.

Increase heat to medium high. Add onion to pot, and cook about 15 minutes. Add bell pepper, celery, and garlic, cook 5 more minutes. Stir occasionally so everything cooks evenly.

Add cooked rice, thyme, bay leaves, paprika, red pepper and celery salt to pot and cook, stirring often, 3 minutes.

Add tomatoes and chicken. Bring to a boil. Reduce heat to medium low, cover the pot and simmer for 15 minutes.

Add shrimp and green onions cook five minutes.

Turn off heat and let everything continue to cook in the pot for 5 more minutes.

Remove lid, stir and eat.

Meatloaf

Ingredients

2 eggs
2/3 cup milk
2 teaspoons salt
1/4 teaspoon ground black pepper
3 slices bread, crumbled or crushed crackers
1 1/2 pounds ground beef (or whatever ground meat)
1 onion, chopped
1 cup shredded Cheddar cheese (optional)
1/2 cup shredded carrot (optional)
1/4 cup brown sugar (optional)
1/4 cup ketchup
1 tablespoon yellow mustard (optional)

Instructions

Preheat oven to 350 degrees F.

Whisk eggs, milk, salt, and ground black pepper in a

large bowl. Add crumbled bread and stir until

dissolved. Chop up the onion and
carrot into very small pieces.

Mix ground beef, onion, Cheddar cheese, and carrot into bread mixture; transfer mixture to a 9x5-inch loaf pan.

Combine brown sugar, ketchup, and mustard in a small bowl; spread over meat mixture. Bake in the preheated oven until no longer pink in the center, 1 to 1 1/4 hours.

Fish

Salmon Spinach & White Beans

Ingredients

Salmon fillets (or any fish)
2 teaspoons plus 1 tablespoon olive oil, divided
1 teaspoon seafood seasoning
1 garlic clove, minced
1 can (15 ounces) cannellini beans, rinsed and drained
1/4 teaspoon salt
1/4 teaspoon pepper
1 package (8 ounces) fresh spinach
1 Lemon

Instructions

Preheat broiler. Rub fillets with 2 teaspoons oil; sprinkle with seafood seasoning. Place on a greased rack of a broiler pan. Broil
5-6 in. from heat 6-8 minutes or until fish just begins to flake easily
with a fork.

Meanwhile, in a large skillet, heat remaining oil over medium heat. Add garlic; cook 15-30 seconds or until fragrant.

Add beans, salt and pepper, stirring to coat beans with garlic oil. Stir in spinach until wilted. Serve salmon with spinach mixture and lemon wedges.

Note: you can use any vegetable that you have in place of the Spinach.

Baked Fish

Ingredients

1 -1 1/2 pound tilapia fillet (or cod, haddock, or any other mild fish)
4 tablespoons butter, melted
2 teaspoons lemon juice
2 teaspoons of minced garlic
1 teaspoon sugar
1/2 teaspoon pepper
1/2 teaspoon thyme
1 tablespoon parsley
1/3 cup breadcrumbs or crushed crackers

Ingredients

Preheat oven to 425. Lightly grease or spray a 13" x 9" (or larger)
baking dish.

Rinse fish filets and pat dry in a paper towel.
Spray or grease a baking dish with butter.

Set the fish in a single layer in the prepared baking dish.

In a small bowl, combine melted butter, lemon juice, garlic, sugar, pepper, thyme and parsley. Stir well.

Pour evenly over fish filets.

Sprinkle with the breadcrumbs.

Bake at 425 for about 20 minutes or until filets are opaque and flakey

Tuna Noodle Casserole

Ingredients

12 ounces medium egg noodles (cooked and drained)
2 cups green peas (cooked)
2 cans cream of mushroom soup
1/2 cup milk
1 1/2 cups sharp cheddar cheese
2 (6-ounce) cans tuna (drained and flaked)
1/2 teaspoon salt (or to taste) Salt and pepper (to taste)
1 cup breadcrumbs
2 tablespoons butter (melted)

Instructions

Heat oven to 350 F.
Spray a 2 1/2 to 3-quart casserole dish with nonstick spray or crease it with butter.

Cook the pasta by the direction on the box. Drain the pasta.

Combine the noodles, peas, soup, milk, cheese, and tuna. Add salt and freshly ground black pepper, to taste. Spoon into the prepared baking dish.

Put breadcrumbs with butter and sprinkle over

the top or the casserole.

Bake for 15 to 20 minutes, until hot and bubbly and crumbs are browned.

Salads

Cucumber Salad

Ingredients

2 small cucumbers, thinly sliced
1/2 small red onion, thinly sliced
1 large tomato, halved and sliced
3 tablespoons mayonnaise
1 tablespoon white vinegar
1/4 teaspoon salt
1/2 teaspoon black pepper

Instructions

In a medium bowl, toss together the cucumbers, red onion and tomato.

Stir in the mayonnaise, vinegar, salt and pepper until coated. Cover and refrigerate for at least 1 hour before serving.

Caprese Salad

Ingredients

1 Carton Cherry Tomatoes
1 pound fresh mozzarella, Chop into Cubes or Pearls
10-15 leaves (about ½ a small bunch) fresh basil
Extra-virgin olive
oil, for drizzling
Balsamic Vinegar,
for drizzling Salt
and pepper

Instructions

Wash the Cherry tomatoes.

Slice the Cherry tomatoes in half.

Cube the mozzarella, chop the basil and mix all together.

Drizzle the salad with extra-virgin olive oil, Balsamic Vinegar and season with salt and pepper, to taste.

Three Bean Salad

Ingredients

1 (15 ounce) can green beans
1 (15 ounce) can yellow wax beans
1 (15 ounce) can kidney beans, drained and rinsed
1 onion, sliced into thin rings
3/4 cup white sugar
2/3 cup distilled white vinegar
1/3 cup vegetable oil
1/2 teaspoon salt
1/2 teaspoon black pepper
1/2 teaspoon celery seed

Instructions

Chop or slice the onion very thin.

Mix together green beans, wax beans, kidney beans, onion, sugar, vinegar, vegetable oil, salt, pepper, and celery seed.

Let set in refrigerator for at least 6 hours.

Side Dishes

Mashed Potatoes

Ingredients

2 pounds Russet potatoes, peeled and quartered (about half a bag)
4 tablespoons butter
1 cup milk
Salt and pepper to taste

Instructions

Peel the potatoes and cut them into smaller pieces.

Bring a pot of salted water to a boil.
Add potatoes and cook until tender but still firm, about 15 minutes; drain.

In a small saucepan heat butter and milk over low heat until butter is melted.

Using a potato masher or electric beater, slowly blend milk mixture into potatoes until smooth and creamy.

Season with salt and pepper to taste.

Mac Salad

Ingredients

1 Pound macaroni
2 Tablespoon apple cider vinegar
2 carrots, shredded
1 small onion, finely chopped
2 1/2 cups Mayonnaise
1/4 cup milk
2 teaspoon sugar
Salt and pepper, to taste

Instructions

Cook macaroni according to package directions. Drain well and place macaroni in a large bowl.

While macaroni is still hot, sprinkle on vinegar and add carrot and onion. Toss together until well combined.

Allow to cool for about 10- 15 minutes. In a separate, smaller bowl, whisk together the mayo, milk and sugar.

Add the mayonnaise mixture into the macaroni until all of the noodles are coated evenly.

Add salt and pepper to taste.

Cover and refrigerate at least 4 hours (best if overnight).

Gently stir before serving adding a little more milk if needed, no more than a tablespoon or two.

White Rice

Ingredients

1 Cup long grain rice
2 cups water
1 teaspoon salt
1 teaspoons butter (optional)
½ teaspoon white vinegar (optional)

Instructions

In a sauce pan with a good fitting lid bring water, salt, butter and vinegar to a boil (don't have to use optional ingredients).

The salt and butter are for added flavor. The vinegar helps to keep the grains separate and you will not be able to taste it.

Once the water is boiling add the rice. Cover and reduce the heat to medium low. You will know your temperature is correct if a little steam is visible leaking from the lid. A lot of steam and your heat is too high.

Cook for 20 minutes. Don't lift lid off pot while cooking.

After 20 minutes remove from heat and fluff with a fork.

Zucchini, Tomatoes & Onions

Ingredients

3 tablespoons olive oil
4 small   zucchini
1 small onion
1 medium tomato
fresh basil or dried basil, to taste salt and pepper to taste
Parmesan cheese

Instructions

Cut the zucchini in
bite size pieces.
Chop the onion.
Dice the tomato.
Heat the olive oil in a heavy skillet.

Cook the zucchini and onion until tender and lightly browned, about
20 minutes.

Add the rest of the ingredients and cook until the juices thicken a little, about 5 or 10 minutes.

Serve with grated parmesan cheese.

Oven Roasted Squash

Ingredients

1 Butternut squash (or acorn or spaghetti squash)
olive oil
salt
black pepper

Instructions

Preheat oven to 400 degrees Fahrenheit.

Clean the squash and then cut into slices lengthwise to uniform thickness, about 1/4 of an inch.

Place on kitchen sheet pan and drizzle

with olive oil. Sprinkle with salt and black

pepper.

Place in oven and cook until tender, about 15 minutes.

Remove from oven and serve warm.

Baked Potatoes

Ingredients

4 large Russet potatoes
1/4 cup olive oil
1 tablespoon salt

Instruction

Preheat the oven to 425 degrees. Wash and dry the potatoes.

Pierce the potato 2-3 times with a fork. Rub oil all over the potatoes.

Rub salt all over the potatoes.

Place the potatoes on a baking sheet and bake for about 45 minutes.

Serve with butter, cheese, chives, sour cream.

Baked Sweet Potatoes

Ingredients

3 – 6 Medium Sweet Potatoes

6 Tablespoons of Butter
Salt and Pepper

Instructions

Heat oven to 400 degrees. Wash the sweet potatoes.

Pierce each sweet potato several times with a fork.

Place the sweet potatoes on a baking sheet lined with foil or parchment paper.

Bake until tender, about 45 minutes. They will be soft when you poke them with a fork.

Make a slit in the top of each sweet potato.

Top with a tablespoon of butter and season with salt and pepper.

Sandwiches

Egg Salad Sandwiches

Ingredients

6 eggs
1/3 cup mayonnaise
1 teaspoon yellow mustard
1/4 cup chopped
green onion salt
and pepper to
taste
1/4 teaspoon paprika

Instructions

Place egg in a saucepan and cover with cold water.

Bring water to a boil and immediately remove from

heat. Cover and let eggs stand in hot water for 10 to 12

minutes. Remove from hot water, cool, peel and chop.

Place the chopped eggs in a bowl, and stir in the mayonnaise, mustard and green onion.

Season with salt, pepper and paprika.

Stir and serve on your favorite bread or crackers.

Hard Boiled Eggs

Ingredients

Eggs
Water
Salt

Instructions

Place your raw eggs in a medium saucepan and cover with at least 2 inches of cold water. Add 1 tablespoon of salt. Place the pan over high heat until it reaches a boil. Turn off heat, cover and let it sit for 13 minutes.

After exactly 13 minutes, remove the eggs from the pan and place them in an ice-water bath and let them cool for five minutes.

Carefully crack the eggs shells (making sure the majority of the shell is cracked).

Begin removing the shells. The ice-water bath will "shock" the membrane in between the egg-white and the egg shell, loosening the shell and allowing you to peel it off in nearly one piece.

As needed, you can dip the egg (as you are peeling it) in and out of the water to remove any slivers of shell.

Tuna Salad Sandwiches

Ingredients

2 cans (6 oz each) tuna in water
1 medium stalk celery (optional)
1 small onion
½ cup mayonnaise
1 teaspoon lemon juice
¼ teaspoon salt
¼ teaspoon pepper
8 slices bread

Instructions

Drain the tuna in a strainer in the sink. Chop the celery to measure 1/2 cup.

Peel and chop the onion to measure 1/4 cup.

In a medium bowl, mix the tuna, celery, onion, mayonnaise, lemon juice, salt and pepper.

Spread tuna mixture on 4 bread slices. Top with remaining bread slices.

Pasta

Lasagna

Ingredients

1 pound lean ground beef or whatever meat you want
1 (32 ounce) jar spaghetti sauce
32 ounces cottage cheese
3 cups shredded mozzarella cheese
2 eggs
1/2 cup grated Parmesan cheese
2 teaspoons dried parsley salt to taste
ground black pepper to taste
9 lasagna noodles
1/2 cup water

Instructions

In a large skillet over medium heat brown the ground beef. Drain the grease. Add spaghetti sauce and simmer for 5 minutes. In a large bowl, mix together the cottage cheese, 2 cups of the mozzarella cheese, eggs, half of the grated Parmesan cheese, dried parsley, salt and ground black pepper.

To assemble, in the bottom of a 9x13 inch baking dish evenly spread 3/4 cup of the sauce mixture. Cover with 3 uncooked lasagna noodles, 1 3/4 cup of the cheese mixture, and 1/4 cup sauce. Repeat layers twice. Top with 3 noodles, pour on the remaining sauce, remaining mozzarella and Parmesan cheese. Add 1/2 cup water to the edges of the pan. Cover with aluminum foil.

Bake in a preheated 350 degree oven for 45 minutes. Uncover and bake an additional 10 minutes. Let stand 10 minutes before serving.

Cut into squares and freeze a couple in quart freezer bags. Pull out and reheat in microwave or oven.

Spaghetti Sauce with Pasta

Ingredients

1 pound ground beef (or any ground meat)
salt and freshly ground black pepper , to taste
1 medium onion, chopped
15 ounces tomato sauce
6 ounces tomato paste
1/2 teaspoon Italian seasoning
1 Tablespoon dried parsley flakes
2 teaspoons minced garlic or 1 teaspoon garlic powder
1 Tablespoon Worcestershire sauce
1 Tablespoon sugar
1 cup water
1/4 cup fresh basil leaves
Spaghetti or Pasta of your choice

Instructions

Season ground beef with salt and pepper. In a large skillet, add the beef and chopped onion and brown.

Drain excess grease.

Add tomato sauce, tomato paste, Italian seasoning, parsley, basil, garlic powder, crushed red pepper, Worcestershire, and sugar to the skillet.

Stir well to combine and bring to a boil. Add water and stir well. Reduce heat and simmer for at least 30 minutes.

Cook the Spaghetti noodles based on the instructions on the box.

One-Pot Penne with Zucchini and Parmesan

Ingredients

2 Medium zucchini
Coarse salt and
freshly ground pepper
8 ounces penne pasta
3 tablespoons extra-virgin olive oil
1/3 cup grated Parmesan
1/2 teaspoon minced garlic
1/4 teaspoon red-pepper flakes

Instructions

Shred zucchini on the large holes of a box grater. (You should have about 4 cups.)

Toss with 1/2 teaspoon salt in a colander set over a bowl. Let stand 10 minutes.

Meanwhile, cook pasta in a pot of generously salted boiling water until al dente. Drain pasta directly over zucchini in colander set in sink.

Transfer both to pot; toss with olive oil, Parmesan, garlic. Season with coarse salt and freshly ground pepper. Serve, dressed with more oil and cheese.

Shrimp Pasta Primavera

Ingredients

4 ounces uncooked angel hair pasta
8 jumbo shrimp, peeled and deveined
6 fresh asparagus spears, trimmed and cut into 2-inch pieces
1/4 cup olive oil
2 garlic cloves, minced
1/2 cup sliced fresh mushrooms
1/2 cup chicken broth
1 small plum tomato, peeled, seeded and diced
1/4 teaspoon salt
1 tablespoon basil, oregano, thyme and parsley
1/4 cup grated Parmesan cheese

Instructions

Cook pasta according to package directions.

Meanwhile, in a large skillet, cook the shrimp and asparagus in oil for 3-4 minutes or until shrimp turn pink.

Add garlic; cook 1 minute longer. Add the mushrooms, broth, tomato, salt; simmer, uncovered, for 2 minutes. Drain pasta.

Add the pasta and seasoning to skillet; toss to coat. Sprinkle with cheese.

58

Breakfast Anytime

Potatoes with Spinach and Eggs

Ingredients

4 large potatoes, peeled and cut into small cubes
½ Tablespoon oil
Knob of butter
1 onion, thinly sliced
Salt and freshly ground black pepper
Fresh Spinach, washed, dried and chopped (or cooked frozen spinach)
12 cherry tomatoes, cut in half
4 large eggs
Cheese for Topping (optional)

Instructions

Place the potatoes in a saucepan with salted water and bring to the boil. Reduce to simmer and cook until tender. This will take about 6 minutes. Drain.

Meanwhile heat a large frying pan. Add the oil and butter. When the butter has melted add in the onion and fry until softened, about 8 minutes.

Add the potatoes, season and cook until golden. Add in the spinach and cook until wilted or heated through. Toss the tomatoes on top. Remove from the heat and make 4 dips in the potato mixture. Crack an egg into each dip. Breakup the cheese and dot it around the eggs. Cover and return to a medium heat.

Cook until the eggs are done to your liking, about 6 minutes.

Desserts

Baked Rice Pudding

Ingredients

4 large eggs
3/4 cup sugar
3 cups milk
1 cup heavy whipping cream
2 teaspoons vanilla
2 teaspoons ground cinnamon
3 cups cooked rice, cooled (leftover rice works great!)
1 cup raisins

Instructions

Preheat oven to 350 degrees F.

Beat the eggs and sugar together. Slowly pour in the milk and cream and mix well.

Add the vanilla and cinnamon and mix well. Add the rice and raisins and stir to combine.

Pour mixture into a greased casserole dish. Any oven-safe dish will work--you can use one pan to bake at least 9x9" big, or smaller individualized serving dishes. Using a 9x9" or slightly larger pan, bake for

30 minutes. Gently stir. Bake for an additional 30-45 minutes or until the top is set and a knife inserted comes out clean.

Peanut Butter Cookies

Ingredients

1 large egg
1 cup creamy peanut butter
1 cup sugar

Instructions

Arrange racks in upper and lower thirds of oven; preheat to 350°F. Line 2 rimmed baking sheets with parchment paper.

Beat egg with a whisk in a medium bowl. Add peanut butter and sugar and whisk until fully incorporated and smooth.

Drop mounds of dough by the tablespoonful onto prepared baking sheets, spacing about 2" apart.

Lightly press tops of cookies with tines of a fork, making a crosshatch pattern.

Bake cookies, rotating trays halfway through, until golden brown, **about** 10–12 minutes. Transfer to a wire rack and let cool slightly. Makes about 2 dozen.

Venison

Stove Top Venison Chili

Ingredients

4 tablespoons unsalted butter
1 red onion, chopped
4 cloves garlic, minced or 2 tablespoons minced garlic
4 tablespoons dark brown sugar
3 cups red wine
4 tablespoons red wine vinegar
4 tablespoons tomato paste
4 cups chicken broth
1 teaspoon ground cumin
1/2 teaspoon cayenne pepper
1/2 teaspoon chili powder
2 tablespoons
chopped fresh
cilantro salt to taste
4 tablespoons oil
10 slices cooked bacon, diced (optional)
1-2 pounds venison stew meat, trimmed and finely diced
1 Can black beans, drained

Instructions

Melt the butter in a large pot over medium heat. Chop the onion into small pieces.

Stir in the onion and garlic, and cook for 3 to 4 minutes. Stir in the brown sugar and cook for 2 to 3 more minutes.

Then stir in the red wine, vinegar, tomato paste, chicken stock, cumin, cayenne pepper, chili powder, cilantro and salt.

Simmer for 30 to 35 minutes, or until the mixture is reduced by about half.

Meanwhile, heat the oil in a large skillet over medium-high heat.

If you are using bacon, stir in the bacon and fry for 3 to 4 minutes, or until the bacon is browned. Move the bacon to one side of the skillet and add the venison to the empty side of the skillet.

Season the meat with salt to taste and cook the meat for 15 minutes, or until well browned. Stir in the beans and toss all together.

Mix everything together thoroughly and let simmer for about 20 more minutes.

Slow Cooker Venison Roast

Ingredients

Venison Roast
1 large onion, sliced
1 tablespoon soy sauce
1 tablespoon Worcestershire sauce
1 tablespoon minced garlic
1/4 teaspoon ground black pepper
1 package dry onion soup mix
1 can cream of mushroom soup

Instructions

Put meat in slow cooker and cover with onion.

Pour in the soy sauce, Worcestershire sauce, garlic salt and pepper.

In a small bowl combine the soup mix and the soup; mix together and then pour mixture over venison.

Cook on Low setting for 6 hours.

Slow Cooker Venison BBQ Sandwiches

Ingredients

Venison Roast
1-1/2 cups ketchup
3 tablespoons brown sugar
1 tablespoon ground mustard
1 tablespoon lemon juice
1 tablespoon soy sauce
1 tablespoon liquid smoke, (optional)
2 teaspoons celery salt
2 teaspoons pepper
2 teaspoons Worcestershire sauce
1 teaspoon onion powder
1 teaspoon garlic powder
1/8 teaspoon ground nutmeg hamburger buns

Instructions

Cut venison roast in half; place in a 5-qt. slow cooker.

In a large bowl, combine the ketchup, brown sugar, mustard, lemon juice, soy sauce, liquid smoke if desired and seasonings.

Pour over venison. Cover and cook on low for 8-10 hours or until meat is tender. Remove roast; cool slightly.

Shred meat with two forks; return to slow cooker and heat through.

Venison Cheeseburger Soup Recipe

Ingredients

1 cup diced potatoes, peeled
½ cup canola oil
1-2 pounds ground venison
1 medium sized chopped onion
1 chopped green bell pepper
1 chopped red pepper
1 cup flour
1 tablespoon Italian seasoning
1 teaspoon salt
1 teaspoon black pepper
1 Carton of beef broth
1 pounds white American cheese, sliced and cubed
1 Bunch chopped Green Onions
1 jalapeños (optional) (Wear gloves to clean and chop)

Instructions

In a large saucepan, add the potatoes and enough water to cover them by about 2 inches.

Bring to a boil over high heat. Lower the heat to medium and simmer, uncovered, until fork-tender, about 15 minutes. Drain and return to the pan. Cover and keep warm.

In a large stockpot, heat the oil over medium-high heat.

When hot, add the venison burger and cook, breaking up the meat slightly with a wooden spoon, until the burger begins to brown, 6 to 10 minutes.

Add the onion and the bell peppers and cook, stirring, for another minute or two.

Add the jalapeños (if you are using them) and then the flour, herb blend, salt, and black pepper.

Cook, stirring until mixed well and thickened, 3 to 4 minutes.
Add the broth, lower the heat to medium, and cook, stirring, until heated through, taking care not to break the meat up too much.

You may also use 1/2 pound of ground venison and 1/2 pound of ground beef if you wish.

Remove the pan from the heat, add the slices of cheese, one at a time, and stir gently until the cheese melts into the soup and the soup becomes creamy. Add the chopped green onions and the potatoes and cook just until heated through. Enjoy.

Venison Taco Pie

Ingredients

2 pounds ground venison
2 envelopes taco seasoning
½ cup water
2 cans crescent rolls
12 ounces sour cream
2 cups shredded sharp cheese

Instructions

Brown and drain venison.

Add taco seasoning and ½ cup water. Mix well.

Pat the 2 cans of crescent rolls into the bottom and up the sides of a greased 9x13 inch cake pan or in a 9" pie plate.

Spread mixed venison on top of crescent rolls. Spread sour cream over venison. Sprinkle with shredded cheese. Bake at 350 degrees for 35-40 minutes.

Let sit for 10 minutes before eating.

Venison Sliders

Ingredients

1 pound ground beef
1 pound ground venison
2 teaspoons extra-virgin olive oil, more for brushing
2 teaspoons salt
1 teaspoon ground cinnamon
1 teaspoon dried oregano
1/2 teaspoon black pepper
1 small bunch fresh flat-leaf parsley, chopped
12 slider buns

Instructions

Combine the beef, venison, oil, salt, cinnamon, oregano, pepper and parsley in a mixing bowl.

Use a spoon, spatula or your hands to blend it thoroughly. Form the meat into twelve 3-ounce sliders, and refrigerate until cooking time.

Brush the sliders with olive oil and cook on a preheated very hot grill or in a nonstick pan for 1 to 2 minutes on each side. Do not overcook. Place the grilled venison sliders on a bun.

Venison Bolognese

Ingredients

1-2 pound ground venison
2 stalks celery, diced
2 carrots, diced
1 onion, diced
1 - 28 ounce can of crushed tomatoes
2 Tablespoons tomato paste
3 Tablespoons olive oil
1 Tablespoons Thyme
2 Tablespoons oregano
1 bunch fresh flat leaf parsley, chopped
2 cups of beef or chicken broth
1 cup of red wine
Salt and pepper
1 box Penne Pasta

Instructions

In a heavy based large pot, brown the venison in batches, using about half the olive oil. It's important to not overcrowd the pan, so the meat browns instead of stews, and to lightly salt each batch as you go. Remove to a bowl once browned.

Add remaining olive oil to the same pan, and brown the onions over medium heat.

Once the onions are see through - translucent, add carrots, celery, thyme and oregano and cook until vegetables have just softened. Return browned venison to the pan, add tomato paste, salt and stir well to combine. Allow to cook one minute.

Add in canned tomatoes, parsley, stock and wine, and stir to combine. Use a wooden spoon to break up tomatoes if necessary.

Cook it until it is as thick as you want it. The longer you cook it the thicker it will get. You can add salt right before serving if needed.

Pasta. Cook your pasta how the box tells you to cook it. Always add a scoop of salt to the water you cook the pasta in and cook pasta Al Dente. It will tell you how on the box.

When the pasta is done spoon the Venison Bolognese sauce over the pasta and top with parmesan cheese.

Venison Stroganoff

Ingredients

1 pound venison, cut into cubes
salt and pepper to taste
1 Tablespoon garlic powder to taste
1 onion, chopped
2 cans cream of mushroom soup
1 (16 ounce) package uncooked egg noodles or bow tie pasta
1 (8 ounce) container sour cream

Instructions

Season venison with salt, pepper and garlic powder to taste. Cook onion in a large skillet; when soft, add venison and brown.

Drain when venison is no longer pink and add soup. Reduce heat to low and simmer.

Meanwhile, bring a large pot of lightly salted water to a boil.

Add noodles and cook for 8 to 10 minutes or until al dente; drain. When noodles are almost done cooking, stir sour cream into meat mixture.

Pour meat mixture over hot cooked noodles and serve.

www.ingramcontent.com/pod-product-compliance
Lightning Source LLC
Chambersburg PA
CBHW080026130526
44591CB00037B/2680